AN INTRODUCTION TO YOGA

AN INTRODUCTION TO YOGA

CLAUDE BRAGDON

GYAN

Published by

Gyan Publishing House
5, Ansari Road
Daryaganj, New Delhi-110002
Phone: 011-47034999, 9811692060
E-mail: books@gyanbooks.com

Distribution Network
gyanbooks.com
India, USA, Canada, UK, Australia

ISBN: 978-93-7169-061-4 (HB)

First Published, 1933

2nd Impression 2025

Printed at: Gyan Press, Delhi.

AN INTRODUCTION TO YOGA
Author: CLAUDE BRAGDON

AN INTRODUCTION TO YOGA

AN INTRODUCTION TO YOGA

BY

CLAUDE BRAGDON

LONDON
KEGAN PAUL, TRENCH, TRUBNER & CO., LTD.
1933

At the first glance which man directs upon himself, he will perceive without much difficulty that there must be a science or an evident law for his own nature, since there is one for all beings, though it is not universally in all, and since even in the midst of our weakness, our ignorance, our humiliation, we are employed only in the search after truth and light. Albeit, therefore, the efforts which man makes daily to attain the end of his researches are so rarely successful, it must not be considered on this account that the end is imaginary, but only that man is deceived as to the road that leads thereto, and is hence in the greatest of privations, since he does not even know the way in which he should walk. The overwhelming misfortune of man is not that he is ignorant of the existence of truth, but that he misconstrues its nature. What errors and what suffering would have been spared us if, far from seeking truth in the phenomena of material nature, we had resolved to descend into ourselves, and had thought to explain material things by man, and not man by material things; if, fortified by courage and patience, we had preserved in the calm of our imagination the discovery of this light which we desire all of us with so much ardour!

DES ERREURS ET DE LA VÉRITÉ,
Louis Claude de St. Martin.

PREFACE

I HAVE never taken lessons in Yoga, much less given them. I have never been to India; nor can I lay claim to that order of scholarship based on exhaustive knowledge which makes possible the deciphering and comparison of texts. I have read only those books—and them uncritically—which would fall naturally into the hands of anyone interested in Oriental philosophy; though I have carefully studied the Yoga Sûtras of Patanjali, the Bhagavad Gita, and certain of the Upanishads. So if this were all, anything which I might write on the subject of Yoga would be at second hand, and probably second rate; but there is another side to the picture, and it is this:

Through that order of freemasonry which brings into relation persons who have a common interest or a common enthusiasm I have met many Hindus in the course of my life and number several among my friends. All of them knew something about Yoga either at first or at second hand, and what they told me had a forthrightness and freshness not to be found in books. To them Yoga was a *living* thing, and not, like India's shrines and temples, only a relic of her glorious past. Something of this livingness I have tried to recapture and render here.

It happened that two of these inheritors of a great tradition had each spent some time in the *âśrama* of a master, and the Yoga practices which they learned there had become a habit of their lives. One of these men was that tea salesman about whom I have written in *Merely Players*. His predicament in a civilization such as ours may be imagined from the fact that the only place he could find for his meditations was a city cemetery after the gates had been closed for the night. The other was Somesh

Chandra Bose, a peripatetic teacher of Indian philosophy, but better known as a lightning calculator. He could add, subtract, multiply and divide with incredible quickness, and on the occasion of our first meeting he extracted the cube root of a number of eighteen digits in a few seconds—almost as soon as the figures were set down.

There was something about these two men which fascinated me: poor and obscure, going from city to city in pursuit of a precarious livelihood, living on almost nothing, subject to many indignities by reason of their dark skins, they were yet self-respecting, self-sufficient, strong, serene, dignified, and full of a *coiled power* which shone from their eyes and betrayed itself not alone in their every movement, but in their stillness as well. All this they attributed to the practice of Yoga.

Of Yoga I accordingly determined to learn the secret, in the only way it can be learned, by taking up the practice of it myself. Along this "small, old path, stretching far away" I have not travelled far; I have gone far enough, however, to have experienced *the inner life of the spirit*—to have sensed a reality unknown to me before. This I discovered to be Yoga's "secret"—what it is all about and what it is all for. It is a secret which is incommunicable: each must discover it for himself. But the process *is* communicable. Told from far back in many a sacred scripture and by many a spiritual teacher; I have tried here to re-tell it in a manner acceptable to modern modes of thought.

For there are many in the world to-day who find themselves at an *impasse*. Materialistic science, having destroyed in them the faith which sustained their forefathers, and the inspiration by which they were fired, gives nothing in its place. Ordinary life does not content them, whether it be of the will, the intellect, or the emotions. They long to experience the inner life of the spirit, but mere vague aspiration gets them nowhere; what they need is something in the nature of *a technique*. Yoga supplies that need.

CLAUDE BRAGDON.

AN INTRODUCTION TO YOGA

I

WITHIN recent years the word Yoga has found place in the Anglo-Saxon vocabulary. To it many strange and even repellent connotations have somehow become attached, despite the fact that the dictionary definition is substantially correct: "Hindu system of philosophical meditation and asceticism designed to effect the reunion of the devotee's soul with the universal spirit."

Perhaps one reason for this general misapprehension is that the dictionary definition involves assumptions counter to the current thought of the day: namely, that there is such a thing as "soul" or as "universal spirit." Another reason is that the word Yoga is associated with a class of unclean and emaciated fanatics given to self-torment sometimes encountered in India by tourists and described in books of travel. A third reason derives from the fact that here in the West the teaching of "Yoga practices" by unscrupulous or unqualified persons has wrought an incalculable amount of secret harm. One of the purposes of this book is therefore to correct a misconception and to sound a warning.

For the understanding of what follows all that the reader needs to know of that Hindu-Aryan cosmo-conception upon which the practice of Yoga is founded is that man is a god in embryo, unaware of his godhead. His aim can therefore be none other than the attainment of that awareness—implicit in the injunction, "Become what thou art!"

Yoga is in its most universal sense the way of attaining to this awareness. In its narrower meaning the word connotes the following of a specific discipline the purpose of which is the merging of the individual consciousness with that of "the universal spirit": it is the technique of *release*—not from life, but into life.

In the East this technique has always been a carefully guarded secret, though accessible to the earnest seeker who possesses the requisite initial qualifications, and is prepared to undergo the necessary discipline. The reason for this secrecy is that the practice of Yoga is fraught with danger. This is because it brings an accession of life, an augmentation of power; and if the character or the organism be not strong enough to sustain the added strain the sort of thing happens which occurs when the voltage of an electrical appliance is increased beyond the limit of its resistance—something analogous to a blow-out or a short-circuit, injuring or wrecking the mechanism.

The more intensive practice of Yoga is not for everybody therefore. So long as one is in the grip of acquisitive ambitions, ungratified desires, of duties unfulfilled and responsibilities not met, such practice would only precipitate an inner warfare more difficult and devastating than that which, by these means, he had hoped to escape. The *wilful* person—that is, one completely immersed in " the-will-to-live "—is at least not dualistic, not torn by contradictory desires, but possesses the aplomb and one-pointedness of the animal. It is man's tragedy, however, as it is his superior good fortune, that this condition cannot last. Eastern religious philosophy recognizes in human life two cycles: the cycle of " identification with objects ", and the cycle of identification with " the great Self without selfishness "—the path of outgoing and the path of return. It is only with this turning from outer to inner that the practice of Yoga becomes effective or should be undertaken—when the soul is " even as a weaned child."

Everyone is a practitioner of Yoga to the extent that his endeavour in whatever field tends to release and bring into operation the super-personal self in him. If his life-activity only feeds and aggrandizes the personal self, he is still on the path of outgoing; if that activity proceeds from the submerged, impersonal self, he is on the path of return. It is this consciousness of a deeper-than-personal self, the recognition of a direction and an aim, and the shaping of his life in accordance therewith which constitutes a man a follower of Yoga: then only will he have need of the more intensive Yoga training in order successfully to continue what is so begun.

The initial objective of Yoga is the *unification* of man's manifold nature; therefore it leaves nothing out of account. And because all dualism, all disorganization of the will, mind, and emotions—and of the body also—have their origin in consciousness (considered not as the aggregate of all the "selves" in man, but as their root or container) Yoga is primarily *the culture of consciousness*.

According to the Eastern teaching consciousness is so far other and deeper than the rational mind, or thinking principle, that it is the activity of the latter which inhibits the natural and free functioning of consciousness. This is implicit in the instruction: "The mind is the slayer of the real: let the disciple slay the slayer." What is meant by this is that the mind must be brought under control, even to the point of arresting its activity altogether. To this task, accordingly, the Yogî addresses himself. The harnessing of the mind is difficult, though the *method* is simple. It consists in concentrating upon some single object, image, or idea to the exclusion of everything else, bringing the attention back whenever it wanders, never letting it be diverted by that stream of associated ideas, so powerful, so automatic, as to seem like the natural and normal functioning of the mind—which it is not.

Until some measure of proficiency in *concentration* is attained, it is useless to attempt *meditation*. This is something quite other than the fixing of the mind on however exalted objects of contemplation, and is the opposite of reverie, in which the fancy roams wherever it wills. Meditation is a condition of *alert passivity* as of listening for inaudible music, or of awaiting the advent of a longed-for guest. The mind, that barking dog, held in leash must be made quiet, and the emotional nature similarly and simultaneously stilled. Meditation, again, is but the vestibule to *contemplation*, about which, transcending as it does normal human experience altogether, nothing at all can here be said.

Before Yoga can be successfully practised the health must be made sound, the senses controlled, the conduct corrected, and the right attitude toward others established. For the achievement of these things no definite rules can be laid down, each must order his life in his own way ; the powerful fiat of the will, " So be it ! " coupled with patient and unceasing effort will bring the desired result to pass.

Although the practice of Yoga is inconsistent with a life of self-indulgence, the Yogî is not an ascetic in the precise meaning of the word, which is " severely abstinent " : the discipline to which he subjects himself need not be—should not be—harsh. Any violence done to nature can have no good effect, for Yoga is itself a natural process. Self-discipline is necessary at all times, but self-torment, never. *Suppression* is at all costs to be avoided ; *expression* is far preferable because from its very nature it is a discharge, and consequently a *purge*—that is, if the determination be firm that it shall so operate ; otherwise it may become a *habit,* and release from the thraldom of habit is the very thing which expression ought to bring about. One should take as one's watchword, "Life ever new through action ever new."

The matter of diet should not be given an exaggerated importance. Though meat and alcohol are probably detrimental to the up-building of that "immortal body" which is the four-dimensional correlative of the physical body, the idea that such things as a bottle of wine or a beefsteak could bar man from his divine inheritance is absurd. Nevertheless, alcohol ministers to no normal physical need, and it is possible to live in health and comfort on the varied products of the vegetable kingdom. Meat and alcohol are *stimulants,* and their elimination from the dietary is therefore recommended; but if the desire for them be so great as to disturb one's serenity, gradual diminishment is better than such sudden and drastic curtailment as would keep the consciousness morbidly centred on such relatively unessential matters. In time the longing for meat and alcohol will cease.

Sexual indulgence, so called, is often classed with drinking and meat eating as inimical to that order of development which the practice of Yoga is assumed to promote; but it can be so classed only when divorced from the emotion of love. If a woman be no more to a man than a drink when he is thirsty or a beefsteak when he is hungry, he will gain nothing from his enjoyment of her but a coarsening of his spiritual fibre. If on the other hand two people enter into this relation charged with a love greater than their own self-love, each wishful of pouring out upon the other all the treasures of tenderness and affection which their hearts hold, their sexual life together will assume an altogether different complexion and be productive of entirely different results. For love, if it be of a certain quality and intensity, brings sexual control and the overcoming of sex-hunger through fulfilments of which lust knows nothing.

Because the physical and psychical effects of sexual intercourse, unlike those attendant upon meat eating and wine drinking, are conditioned by the state of consciousness in which it is entered into, nothing more need be said about it in this connection except that if it disturbs and divides instead of harmonizing and unifying, such intercourse should be avoided. The re-constitution of the entire nature into an organic unity of a superior order, for the recapture of a long-lost and forgotten rapture, is the objective of Yoga, and to the attainment of this objective sexual love may be a fetter or it may be wings.

Man is a seed which he himself must make to sprout, and he must die as a seed in order to live as a tree. Such was perhaps Christ's meaning when He said, " Whosoever will lose his life for my sake the same shall be saved." The loss of life here referred to is that of the personality—the sense of I-ness which alone suffers or can suffer, which alone dies or can die. "For my sake" means for the sake of "the universal spirit" with which it is impossible to associate the idea of suffering or of death.

Yoga is therefore not an additive but a subtractive process, for it is the losing of the I-consciousness, the stripping away of the accumulations of the personal self which interfere with the realization of oneself as an organ of the universal spirit and an agent of its activity. It is of the nature of the personality to be separative and possessive: this separativeness the Yogi strives to overcome by loving; this possessiveness, by giving. It is of the nature of the personality to react violently to persons and events, to like them or dislike them. The Yogî does not resist, retaliate, or react in any manner, save to send forth loving kindness, free from enmity, free from ill will. He neither clings to what is pleasant nor seeks to avoid what is unpleasant; he dramatizes himself as unconditioned in order that he may become so.

It is impossible to proceed far along this particular pathway without somewhere crossing the trail of Buddha and of Christ. The reason is obvious: their aim also was to effect the "reunion of the devotee's soul with the universal spirit" by indicating, in their life and in their teaching, the conduct of life and the condition of consciousness which tend to bring this about.

The latest generalizations in theoretical physics, based on research and discovery, are so far as they go in perfect accord with the ideas upon which Yoga is founded. That the universe is in the nature of a *continuum,* in which forces, forms, and phenomena are alike the result of *an effort toward equilibrium*, is no less a teaching of Eastern philosophy than it is a tentative conclusion of Western physics, the only difference being that science thus far hesitates to posit an Active Intelligent Cause—though its presence is suspected by reason of the amazing mathematical orderliness, the intimations of *design* everywhere in evidence. This appears to be the one key lacking to admit us of the West into that chamber of thought wherein the Yogî sits immemorially in meditation, and one can almost hear the rattle of that key in the lock in these words of Arthur Stanley Eddington, high priest of modern science :

> "We have found a strange footprint on the shores of the unknown. We have devised profound theories to account for its origin. At last we have succeeded in reconstructing the creature that made the footprint. And lo ! it is our own."

Is this not almost equivalent to saying that the cosmos, with all its suns, stars and milky ways, is *the perception of a perceiver,* and that the world without and the world within—cosmos and consciousness—are one and the same?

Such, at any rate, is the concept upon which Yoga is founded: that behind every particular manifestation there is a generalization; that the consciousness of man is a particularized manifestation of a generalized universal consciousness; that the faculties and powers which are his are individualized manifestations of universal forces, and that between the two there is an unbroken continuity and one-to-one correspondence which makes his life one with the Universal Life; his breath one with the Great Breath. All this is implicit in the occult instruction: "As is the great, so is the small; as is the outer, so is the inner: nothing is great, nothing is small"; and it gives meaning to the declaration: "I am *That*!"

But by reason of the identification of his consciousness with his psychic nature or personal self—" a thing of shreds and patches " built by desire and self-will—man has lost his sense of that One Absolute Existence which he essentially *is*. Yoga is the technique of its recapture. It begins therefore with the adjustment of the individual to his social environment on the basis of One Absolute Existence. The Yogî is self-committed to a blameless life because in injuring others he would be injuring himself—not because it is " wicked "; and because in helping others he is helping himself—not because it is " good ". His attitude in matters of this sort is illustrated in perfection by the following anecdote told by Alfred Stieglitz.

There was an organ grinder who used to appear regularly in the street where Stieglitz lived as a boy, and he formed the habit of always giving the man a little money or a bit of food. One day, while seated at table with his parents, Stieglitz heard the familiar strains of the organ, and leaving the company abruptly he hurried out into the street with some food and a cup of coffee for his friend. On his return his mother reproached him for interrupting the meal for such an errand, and deserting his parents who were so fond of him. When she had finished Stieglitz said, " Mother, do you know who that man was ? " " Why no, some beggar of an organ grinder I suppose ; who was he ? " she answered. " Mother," responded Stieglitz, " that man was myself."

The Yogî, having organized his outer life in accordance with this conception (that he is Everyman because all are One Absolute Existence) next turns his consciousness *inward,* and in the rapt stillness of meditation endeavours to organize his inward life in similar fashion. Through thought-control he purifies his psychic nature, thereby releasing himself from the desire-net in which he was enmeshed. This re-polarization of consciousness has repercussions in every part of man's manifold nature, releasing new faculties and powers by organizing that " subtle body " through and by means of which they manifest.

For the true constitution of man is quite other than that shown in the anatomy books. Eddington, in *The Nature of the Physical World,* calls attention to the vast discrepancy between such a thing as a table as it seems to sensuous perception—a static and a solid object—and as revealed to the mind of the physicist—an aggregate of whirling electrons of no substantiality whatever. An analogous difference subsists between the physical body of man and his subtle body, though the two are interwoven and interrelated, and occupy the same space, one being three dimensional and the other four dimensional.

A feature of this subtle body is the *Chakras* or centres, through and by means of which *Prâna,* the universal life-energy, is transformed and transmitted from vehicle to vehicle. Conceive of man as a walking tree; its stem the spine, its root the basic centre, its summit the crown centre, and the other centres flowers attached to the parent stem by stems of their own. This tree is vitalized from its root centre by the sap of *Kundalini,* or serpentine fire, which rising flows into every branch, twig, flower; it is nourished no less by *Prâna,* absorbed through the centres and taken in with the breath, as a tree is nourished by rain and sun.

Through the practice of Raja Yoga—"the royal road to union"—the centres become active at the right time and in the right way, like flowers opening to the sun. Hatha Yoga, which awakens them artificially by means of physical exercises, should never be attempted by the novice. Innumerable psychic ills, of which many persons, particularly women, are in these days the victims—visions, voices, automatic writing, possession, obsession, dissociation of personality and manias of one sort and another—are due to the irregular and premature awakening of the centres without the ability or knowledge to cope successfully with the resultant conditions. If those who are thus afflicted go for help to the representatives of a science which knows nothing of the occult they are apt to be regarded as pathological subjects ; and treated as such, this they soon become. In the majority of cases this awakening of the centres has been brought about unconsciously and as it were automatically by some order of introversion—the inward turning of consciousness upon itself as a result of fear, frustration, lack of sympathy and understanding on the part of others, or some violence done to the love-nature. Sometimes, however, such psychic disorganization is the result of practices taught or recommended by ignorant or unscrupulous teachers of Yoga. There is one sure way whereby these fakers may be known: if they require money for their instruction that fact alone condemns them; for the true Yogi obeys the occult law that material profit may not be derived from the bestowal of spiritual gifts. His metaphorical begging bowl may perchance be filled by the grateful recipient of such gifts, but he is not supposed to solicit such beneficences—to demand, much less.

II

THERE are different kinds of Yoga, corresponding to differences in human temperament; but these various disciplines are closely interrelated and ultimately merge into one another, as pathways up the side of a mountain merge into the single pathway to the peak. Here are the names of the more important Yoga systems, with a rough and ready characterization of each :

1.	Raja Yoga.	Union by Will.
2.	Hatha Yoga.	Union by Courage.
3.	Gnana Yoga.	Union by Knowledge.
4.	Bhakti Yoga.	Union by Love.
5.	Karma Yoga.	Union through Service.
6.	Mantra Yoga.	Union through Speech.

Of these Raja Yoga is held in highest esteem, and in this book will receive the most extended consideration. It may be said to include all other Yogas—in its results, not in its practices—and it will perhaps eventually find its greatest use and justification here in the West. Hatha Yoga is in a way directly antithetical to Raja Yoga, yet supplementary to it. But Hatha Yoga is a discipline to which we of the West are not well suited; an element of danger is involved in it; therefore its practice is not recommended. These two Yogas will be dealt with later in conjunction, after the remaining four have been briefly described.

Gnana Yoga is a discipline whereby, through an intention of consciousness upon the ephemeral world, it is *seen through,* and the permanent wisdom of *Atman*—the Eternal Self—is arrived at. Its first stage is the discernment of *true values:* the distinguishing of the real from the transitory; its second is the transcending of worldly knowledge, indifference to the sorrows and joys of the psychic or personal self; its third is *Mukti*, release from that self, emancipation from rebirth, and union with the universal spirit.

Bhakti Yoga is the Yoga of devotion; and of them all it is the swiftest and most ecstatic. It is, however, only for the few—those whose greatness lies in loving. In Bhakti means and end are one and not different; love is not cultivated for the sake of a more abundant life, but life is lived for the sake of loving. The effect of this is the transmutation of human passion and emotion into its loftiest and most universal expression. This is never the path of renunciation because the Bhakti gives up all gladly for the sake of love.

Karma Yoga is the Yoga of service—of salvation by works in contradistinction to salvation by faith—faith in love, in the case of the Bhakti. Those altruistic, truly philanthropic and public-spirited individuals which Western civilization develops in considerable numbers follow, all unconsciously, the Karma Yoga path. Until they supplement Karma Yoga with Raja Yoga, however, they will experience only the inner peace which attends the doing of good works, and not " the bliss of Brahman ".

Mantra Yoga is likely to remain a mystery to persons immersed in Western modes of thought; incredulous, therefore, of the occult properties and potencies of *sound*. Mantra Yoga is based upon the knowledge that certain sounds, uttered in a particular manner, and with a definite intention of consciousness upon them, are dynamic, creative, and precipitate *a release of force*. A prayer, holy verse, sacred or mystic word, recited or contemplated during his devotions, constitute for the Mantra Yogi " the chariot which bears him to the world of Brahman ". Generally speaking, Mantra Yoga is employed as an adjunct to other practices under one or more of the other Yoga disciplines. Music is a part of Mantra Yoga;

singers and actors are unconscious practitioners of it, since they induce changes of consciousness in themselves and others by the production of tones, the utterance of words in a certain manner.

Coming now to the consideration of Raja Yoga and Hatha Yoga, the fundamental difference between them consists in this: in Hatha Yoga, by means of certain physical exercises, disciplinary both of the mind and of the body, changes are induced in consciousness which raise it above its normal level; in Raja Yoga, through the practice of meditation, consciousness "raises" itself. Hatha Yoga starts from the premise that the *sine qua non* is a healthy body and one which is under perfect control. As the body is brought more and more under control the mind increasingly asserts its sway over the body, and the mind in turn comes under the domination of the spiritual nature. In other words, Hatha Yoga starts from "below" and works upward, while Raja Yoga starts from "above" and works downward. The two are, however, so intimately related that there is a point at which they merge into one another and become one. Beyond this bare statement nothing further need be said about Hatha Yoga for the reason that all information gathered through hearing or reading about it is without practical value, and dangerous if acted upon. Hatha Yoga should never be undertaken save under the constant observation of a teacher, and in the West there are none possessing the necessary qualifications. Moreover, no one who is not qualified should attempt this practice, and one is no judge of one's own fitness.

Raja Yoga, on the contrary, can be practised with safety by any normal, healthy, sincere and earnest person *if actuated by the right motive*, because in that case consciousness itself is made to perform the office of master, the awakened and sensitized *intuition* enabling one to determine how far to go in any given direction and what next to undertake. There is only one danger-point, and that is where Raja Yoga and Hatha Yoga impinge on one another. This has to do with " the control of the life-currents " and involves the regulation of the breath.

Prânâyâma, by reason of its having to do first of all with the control of breathing, which is a physical function, would seem to be a Hatha Yoga practice, for Hatha Yoga is based on physical exercises ; but there is something unique about breath and the act of breathing which relates *Prânâyâma* to Raja Yoga, making it part of that discipline too. Raja Yoga, be it remembered, is *the culture of consciousness.* Now the life-breath is so inextricably bound up with consciousness that it is difficult to disentangle the two : when the first breath animates the lungs of a new-born infant its life truly begins, consciousness enters; and with the cessation of the act of breathing at the moment of death, consciousness departs. Lacking the breath, mind and senses cannot function. Breath is indeed lord of the body and for that reason Brahma is said to assume in the body the form of breath. This being so, the devotee of Raja Yoga must needs concern himself with breath-culture along with the culture of consciousness, in which case *Pránáyáma* becomes a Raja Yoga practice, despite the fact that it is a physical exercise. It is at this point that the two Yogas meet.

Pránáyáma begins with the regulation of the breath for the purpose of obtaining control over the life-currents. From the simplest and most natural exercises Hatha Yoga proceeds to the most difficult and austere. In this book the initial exercise is the only one which will be—or need be—given. The further modifications of the breath will ensue naturally in the right sequence, *following* changes of consciousness. It is said that Swami Vivekânanda came to regret what he had told concerning *Prânâyâma* in his excellent book, *Raja Yoga,* after having learned that the following of his instructions had done harm by reason of psychological and physiological peculiarities which he, because he was a Hindu, failed to take into account, although in this very book he himself had written : " The way the Hindus practise this would be very difficult for this country, because they do it from their childhood, and their lungs are prepared for it."

Indeed, it would be about as difficult to learn *Prânâyâma* from books as it would be to learn lion taming—and about as dangerous to attempt it. Though this is only a figure of speech it is particularly apposite : the air taken in by the lungs is the source of the greater part of the life energy ; if therefore the breath be feeble, as it is ordinarily, that energy will lie asleep as it were, like a lion in its cage ; but let the supply of air be augmented, conserved, and a rhythm imparted to its in-flow and out-flow, the life-energy will be as a lion aroused, beating against the bars of its cage, trying to escape. Having awakened this mysterious force, with no knowledge of how to control or direct it, there is danger of falling a prey to grave disorders, physical and psychical, even to the point of going insane.

The following *Prânâyâma* exercise is the only one which may be practised with safety by anybody, therefore it is the only one which will be given here. There is nothing forced or unnatural about it ; by these means a correct habit of breathing may be established in place of the light irregular breathing customary to almost everyone.

Having assumed the posture of meditation—presently to be described—draw in the breath steadily for the space of four seconds, hold it for sixteen, and expel it for eight, silently and so steadily that it would not disturb a feather held directly underneath the nose. The air should be inhaled and expelled through each nostril alternately. The thumb or forefinger may be used for the closing of the nostrils, and the time may be determined by counting.

This exercise should be performed about ten times at the beginning of every period of meditation, for by these means the habit of correct breathing will gradually become established. Further modifications will ensue in the course of time without thought or effort, in conformity with changes in consciousness.

In India certain symbolic words are used for counting. The mental repetition of the sacred syllable " Om " is recommended, for it quiets the nerves. The nerve centre which controls the respiratory organs is like a master switch, it controls also the other nerve centres.

Prânâyâma is more than the control of the breath, it is the control of the life-currents through and by means of the breath. In Hatha Yoga this is itself an objective, but the aim of Raja Yoga is other: consciousness is not centred on the machine, but on the Self, its maker and master. The control of all the physical functions is handed over to the aroused *spiritual will*, the organ of which is the *intuition*, the mind being used not to inaugurate but to register and remember. So long as the spiritual will is in command, danger does not exist; it enters only when the mind is permitted to transcend its proper function.

In performing this one *Prânâyâma* exercise more than correct breathing is achieved: it is an exercise also in *attention*, which is preliminary to meditation proper. Meditation of one sort or another is common to all Yoga disciplines, but in Raja Yoga it is of supreme importance, because in it the culture of consciousness is carried on at its source—in the so-called unconscious. The conditions under which meditation is undertaken constitute a success-factor of great importance; therefore it will be well to describe the conditions most favourable.

Ideally, the *place* of meditation should be out of doors: pleasant, secluded, quiet, and dedicated solely to this purpose. For city dwellers, however, and for those forced to endure inclement climates, one's own bedroom, in default of a better place, will answer. The best time is after the morning bath (a cold one if the constitution will stand it), as soon after sunrise as possible, for then the air is pure and the solar vibrations positive. Midday, sunset, and midnight, though less favourable times, are well enough—or any time of the day or night, for that matter. But whatever time is chosen it should be adhered to: if possible, meditation should be always at the same hour and in the same place. The clothing (if any) should be light and loose, of cotton or linen preferably.

Correct posture is as necessary for the successful practice of meditation as correct form is necessary for tennis or golf. That posture is the best in any given case which continues to be comfortable for the greatest length of time, so long as it is also erect and symmetrical—erect, that is, in the sense of having the chest, neck, and head in one vertical line. The body should never be permitted to collapse: to sit crookedly and try to meditate is bad.

If the position can be maintained without discomfort, an admirable posture is the one in which Buddha is so often represented: the body straight and at ease, the legs folded as one folds the arms, or if that be too difficult, crossed merely, the arms relaxed from the shoulders, the hands, with thumbs touching, lightly clasped in the lap. Those who find this posture unnatural may sit in a chair in the attitude in which the sculptors of ancient Egypt were wont to represent her priest-kings: the legs together, feet parallel, arms relaxed, the extended hands resting, palms downward, on the thighs.

Somesh Chandra Bose, mentioned in the Preface, showed the author the posture considered in India superior to any other, and favoured by his master, a great Yogi: the body erect, resting on the folded and interlocked legs and feet, the arms and hands similarly folded and interlocked behind the back. Bose declared that with practice this posture could be maintained without fatigue for hours on end, and possessed every advantage. The author, however, finding himself unable even to assume it, is of the opinion that this attitude is suited only to those who are accustomed from childhood to squatting on the ground instead of sitting in chairs.

These simple instructions with regard to place and posture are all-sufficient; indeed, a single passage in the Bhagavad Gita tells everything that needs to be known in even more succinct form:

> In a pure place, established in a fixed seat of his own, by himself . . . neither much raised nor very low . . . in a secret place by himself. There he should practise Yoga for the purification of the self. Holding the body, head, and neck erect, immovably steady, looking fixedly at the point of the nose with unwandering gaze.

Having assumed the chosen posture for meditation, and by means of the exercise already given having established the proper inflow and outflow of the breath, let the practitioner of Yoga become as quiet and relaxed as possible, making sure of the absence of all muscular and nervous tension. Igor Sikorsky, the first Russian to build and fly a heavier-than-air machine in his own country, was brought to earth on his very first exhibition flight by engine trouble which he afterwards traced to the presence of a mosquito in a feed-valve. Any little bodily tension may act in the same disastrous way in meditation—as an interference, that is, with the free and harmonious flow of the life-currents.

Concentration is the first thing to be acquired: it is useless to attempt meditation until one has learned to concentrate the mind. Quiet, at ease, strive to fix the thought on some single image or idea, *and keep it there*. Repeated failure will demonstrate how difficult a thing this is to do; the attention is sure to wander, and must be brought back again and again. To control the mind in this way is perhaps no more difficult, really, than to drive a golf ball into a distant hole or to carom a pool ball into a distant pocket, but at first it will seem immensely hard because it involves an inward-turning of the mind, new to experience.

The *subject* of concentration is not, at this stage, of great importance, for this is a gymnastic, pure and simple: one may take an actual object, a mental image, an idea, a text, a word, a sound, a colour, but once the choice is made everything else must be shut out. A novice's first experiments in concentration will resemble the author's first ascent in a captive balloon: it seemed as though struck by a tornado by reason of the resistance of the anchoring rope, though before the rope had run out to its full length there appeared to be no wind at all. Only after the attempt is made to fix and hold the mind does one become conscious of a constantly-blowing strong wind of thoughts and images therebefore unregarded because unopposed. The mind must be brought back whenever it wanders, and held with steadiness. Improvement will come little by little, and the exercise ought not to be intermitted even for a day. The same law applies to this as to any physical gymnastic: an acrobat or a juggler if he neglects his practice for a single day must devote at least twice the time to it the following day in order not to lose his proficiency.

Until the mind can be controlled it cannot be stilled, and this stilling of the mind, the emptying of it of every thought and image is the next thing to be attempted after a certain amount of power of concentration has been attained. "Meditation with seed" is that in which there is still the distillation of the essence of objectivity. "Meditation without seed" is that in which that essence alone remains, and where there is a cessation of all movement. These may seem only meaningless phrases, but they indicate definite stages of super-consciousness. It is manifestly impossible to give any intelligible notion of a state of consciousness in which all forms, together with the field of knowledge, vanish. From the standpoint of ordinary life in the world this highest form of meditation (*Samâdhi*) can be likened only to a sleep or trance condition. It is, however, the very reverse of this: so fully awake and aware is the spiritual man on planes of being which defy definition or description that it is ordinary life in the world which is dream-like and unreal by comparison; for he has pierced the veil of *Mâyâ* and passed into the light which, like sunlight on morning mist, both made it and made it visible. Non-being is swallowed up in being, and the bliss of Self-realization.

III

REMOTE as Yoga may seem from the subject of sex, it is nevertheless impossible to write about Yoga other than superficially without dealing with its sex-aspect.

For Yoga is *equilibrium,* a balance established between two antithetical activities through their harmonious interrelation. The difference between these activities, whatever their nature or on whatever plane of manifestation, is a *sex* difference, and in the Oriental treatment of the subject this is recognized and frankly expressed. Our own conception of sex is too narrow, too vitiated by ideas of secrecy, sin, and shame to enable us to grasp and appreciate the profound truths behind Oriental imagery and symbols, phallic or otherwise: shame-faced and material-minded, we draw grotesquely erroneous inferences, degrading to ourselves. The Yogi's task is to re-polarize his entire nature and so change its function—to make out of a horse-shoe a horse-shoe magnet—but polarity is sex, and there you are!

Or to put the matter in another way: Yoga is that endless and all-absorbing love affair with God to which all others are initiatory and preparatory; and sex in some form is an indissoluble part of love, even the highest—its rite, its ritual, or else its allegory, its symbol. Coomaraswamy says, "There is nothing with which we can better compare the mystic union of the finite with its infinite ambient . . . than the self-oblivion of earthly lovers locked in one another's arms where 'each is both.'" It is certainly true that the supreme mystical experience has ever found its most intense and eloquent expression in the language of sexual love, from the Songs of Solomon and the outpourings of the Sufi poets to the writings of Saint Teresa and Saint John of the Cross.

The reason for this, strange as it may sound to the ears of puritans, mentalists, body-haters and deniers, is that this mystical experience partakes of the nature of sex-intoxication, though generalized, as it were, and of a quality far other than "the brief pleasure of the frightened in the arms of the frightened." It is as though the universal spirit had given, in the ecstatic moment of sex-fusion and sex-fulfilment, a faint and far-off foretaste of its own bliss-nature, the memory of which should so fire man's imagination and lead him on, that he would never rest content until he had experienced a beatitude to be gained only in the union of his mortal part with its immortal counterpart.

This idea—that within and behind the love of the sexes lies the love of the self for the Self—is part of the *Vedánta* teaching and constitutes the basis of the Brahminical rituals governing marital life wherein the idea is expressed in symbolical form. In marriage it is expected of the Brahmin that he will not give way to sexual excess, but on the other hand learn sexual control; that he will harmonize and bring under the domination of his spiritual will that part of his nature, thus preparing himself for his " forest life " and the austere discipline of Yoga, which carries sexual control to the greatest possible lengths.

Because in Yoga equilibrium is so important, the mind of the aspirant should be free from the obsession either of unsatisfied or of over-indulged desires: as Krishna tells Arjuna, " Verily, Yoga is not for him who eateth too much or who abstaineth to excess." The self-indulgent man is a weakling, but he who desires and acts not is made sick by his own self-engendered poisons. The Yoga method is not, however, one of compromise; equilibrium is not gained through an alternation between debauchery and asceticism, but through a control of the senses, mind, and imagination by means of meditation, which brings into activity the spiritual will, the " body's lord ", master of its every function. If it has been the good fortune of the devotee to have had his spiritual will already aroused by love of the beloved, chastening and disciplining his passional nature, his initiation into the more esoteric mysteries of Yoga will be the easier. Indeed, this love-experience in one form or another—happy or sad, successful or frustrated—is a necessary preliminary to such initiation; for the whole thing is part of a continuous process with phases which everyone must of necessity pass through—a Jacob's ladder no single rung of which may be skipped.

But at a certain point in this ascent everything *reverses*, changes from outer to inner, *involution* replacing *evolution*. This is the point at which, under penalty of *devolution*, man must take his destiny out of the jurisdiction of nature, away from the vicissitudes of outward circumstance, into his own hands. Here also is where Yoga, in its self-conscious form, properly begins. For Yoga is *the path of return* which lies within "the city of Brahman", a world both beyond and interior to that of sensuous perception and rational apprehension.

Now every one of the five senses has its correlative inner sense—sight: clairvoyance; hearing: clairaudience, and so on—and this, its inner sense-mechanism. These inner senses are stimulated into activity by meditation, which is the turning of the consciousness back upon itself, not for self-analysis, but for self-consciousness in the All-Self. The sexual organism has also its inner correlative, and this is bi-polar, because the inner man is androgynous. The sexual problem for the ordinary man or woman arises only at the age of puberty, with the awakening of the sexual nature; the sexual problem of the Yogî, similarly, becomes again acute with the awakening of his bi-polar nature.

The sexual problem of the average man or woman may be stated thus: How shall the sexual life be adjusted to the social life and to life as an individual so that it shall ennoble and enrich instead of disorganize, pollute, or impoverish? For that it can do any or all these things is not to be denied. Everyone must face this problem in his own way and work out his own solution, which can never be according to any man-made, narrowly moralistic formula, for sex is one of those things in which " 'tis man's perdition to be safe." The degree of his success or failure, could it be known, would be the true measure of his spiritual stature, but it can never be known, even to himself, because the factors involved are infinite in number and complexity.

The sexual problem of the Yoga devotee is similar, though not identical, for it involves not the adjustment, merely, of the natural demands of sex, but the mastery of the sexual nature as a preliminary to the dedication of the sexual energy to something unrelated either to pleasure or to procreation ; its translation into another thing altogether. This mastery may be gained either in wedlock or without it, but not through libertinism on the one hand or sex-starvation on the other. It can never be gained at all except through the invoking of the spiritual will, which alone can control the passions. Those who restrain their desires in any other way do so because they are weak enough to be restrained ; and the restraining agent, be it fear, prudence, reason, or what not, usurps its place and governs the unwilling, which is no solution at all. *True love* is the true restrainer because it is itself one aspect of the spiritual will. To some this statement may seem the merest sophistry, paradoxical, fallacious, but anyone who has experienced the strengthening and purifying effect of true love knows it to be a fact—knows that the tides of the blood are indeed obedient to the love-god—that erotomania is cured by Eros. True love, not asceticism, is the true atonement for the sins against sex, of which all, at one time or another, have been guilty.

Yoga does not bring about the weakening of the sexual energy—rather the reverse—but the awakening of the spiritual will enables the Yogî to control and direct that energy—to transmute it, in point of fact. According to the Eastern teaching the energies of the body are stored up in the brain, and the highest of these energies is called *Ojas,* which means " the illuminating or bright." The retention of this in the body strengthens it and prolongs life. That part of human energy which is expressed in sexual passion easily becomes changed into *Ojas*—" It." But here appears to be an *impasse:* if to obtain *Ojas* is so important; if the sexual power is the chief means of supplying it with the renewed energy necessary to maintain it; and if that power is itself developed and maintained by the normal and healthy functioning of the sexual organism—as it is impaired by abuse and excess—how shall the devotee proceed? The Hatha Yoga answer is this: Since the suppression of the first (sex-potency) means the ultimate extinction of the second (*Ojas*), there are some exercises which both maintain and conserve the sex energy; these are called *Mudrâs.* What certain of these practices really effect is the development of the interior bi-polar sexual organism related to the other as clairaudience is related to hearing and clairvoyance to sight—for that every *outer* has its corresponding *inner* is one of the axioms of this science. These exercises should never be undertaken by the novice or except under the instruction and observation of a teacher, but to assure the reader that one of their purposes is the conservation of the sex energy, here is what the Hatha Yoga Pradipika says about the effect of one of these *Mudrás*: "His (the practitioner's) seminal fluid is not emitted even though he be embraced by a young and passionate woman."

Raja Yoga achieves the same result—the development of the androgynous nature—by a different method. Raja Yoga is a quickening of the evolutionary and involutionary process through the culture of consciousness. As the matter under discussion is part of that involutionary process, *meditation* releases the spiritual will which in turn develops the interior sense organs. In this manner the same result is accomplished as by the practice of the *Mudrás*, and in a safe, orderly, and natural manner, rather than by one difficult and dangerous. Raja Yoga is the Yoga of the spiritual will;

Hatha Yoga involves only the exercise of the physical will—it is the Yoga of courage.

There is another way of taking this particular hurdle—by Bhakti Yoga, the way of joy, but it is open only to those who are capable of a love so great and of such a kind that to the "low loving herd" it would not seem like love at all. The adjective sometimes used to characterize this love is "cosmic", meaning universal, or all-embracing; but this suggests something cold and remote, and it is impossible to conceive of love as other than something warm and near. Emerson names this ultimate love "celestial", because it partakes of the divine nature; and this is the better word, because according to the testimony of all the saints and mystics the divine love *is* warm and near.

Bhakti is easier than all the other Yogas, just as to fly is easier than to walk—for those who can! Love, being self-evident, depends on no other truths. The Bhakti has not to suppress any of his emotions or control his thoughts ; he has only to intensify and purify them and direct them toward the object of his adoration. He is bound by no rules, because rules are conditioning and he is unconditioned. Yoga itself is transcended because Yoga is a means to an end, whereas Bhakti is its own fruition, its own means and its own end. Bhakti Yoga is extreme devotion to the Beloved, and the identification of that Beloved with the Self. Every thought, every action, every aspiration is for and toward the Beloved whom the Bhakti beholds everywhere and in everything. The mighty ocean of love having entered into him he desires nothing, grieves not, hates not. Partaking of the nature of love he participates in its perfection, bliss, immortality.

The fundamental difference between Raja Yoga and Bhakti Yoga dwells in this : in the one case the personality is *transcended,* in the other it is *transformed*. The transcending of the personality is necessarily a painful process, because it is the giving up of a lesser thing for the sake of a greater (" whosoever loseth his life for my sake ", etc.): but the transforming of the personality through love is on the contrary a joyful process, because love alone is capable of *glad* sacrifice.

The Beloved, fundamentally, is, and can only be, God (*Iśvara*). But God is everywhere and in all things; all things are infinite and all infinities are equal, so that the phrase, " I go to worship sinful man " is of perfect validity, or even the worship of " a flower in the crannied wall ": it is not the quality of the *object*, but of the *worship*—the love—which is important. Therefore the love of man for woman and of woman for man may be a pathway to liberation, when it transcends the love of persons and becomes the organic activity of the bi-polar, super-personal Self.

Man and woman, because they are one spirit

in two bodies, are in their destiny indissolubly bound up with one another; there is no liberation for either unless it be for both. But to achieve this liberation they must *make one another free,* and the reason that this is so rare and difficult is because the primary instinct of each is, in the name of love, to enslave—and so destroy—one another. The unique merit of salvation through love dwells in the unequalled power of love to effect transformation, regeneration. The difficulty consists in the fact that the first effect of love between the sexes—or in fact of any personal love—is the intensification of the personality which from its very nature is hungry, coercive, possessive. But along with this intensification of the personality comes the power, under the stimulus of love, to effect its transformation; to polarize it spiritually, with the result that the freedom which cannot be had *in,* may be had *through* the personal relation.

In general it may be said that Raja Yoga, which is liberation through and by means of the will, is the man's path; Bhakti Yoga, which is liberation through and by means of the heart, is the woman's path; for love's secret dwelling place is in the heart of the Great Mother, that tree of which every woman is as it were an individual flower. Along this path man may be led by woman if both be courageous enough, sufficiently dedicated and united, if their love be of the right kind and ardency—if they love *enough*, in point of fact. Man may tread this particular path without woman's aid only if through much loving in many lives the woman in him has awakened, for this alone will give him the power to control his passional nature—it is the water which quenches that particular fire.

The reason why woman must lead in this and man must follow is because only with her help can he " redeem " his sexual nature. Man has sinned against love by his sexual irresponsibility, divorcing his sex-life from his love-life, and making his sexual organism a mere agent of sensual gratification. The result of this is that his sexual organism leads a lawless and imperious existence of its own, wild and wolfish like a dog escaped from the leash. Woman has not been able to effect this divorce between her sexual nature and her love nature except rarely, under exceptional circumstances—by reason of the pressure of economic necessity or extreme masculine coercion; and even then it is superficial, the result of her slave-psychology, her tendency to do the thing which is expected of her. Both for biological reasons and for the reason above stated, woman, unless deeply stirred emotionally, has no sexual problem of the kind and to the degree that man has, save as he creates it for her, or as she assumes his own. With her it is more apt to be a social problem created by conventional morality or a part of her love-problem, practically non-existent when divorced from that. In a love-relation her sexual problem becomes acute mainly by reason of man's inability through lust, ignorance, precipitancy, to satisfy the true requirements of her sexual nature, so indissolubly united with her emotional and aesthetic nature, so disseminated, so slow to awaken, so dependent upon the feeling of security, the certainty of affection, caresses and the display of tenderness. In this way he kills the thing he loves, which is her love for him.

Lust is not born of love, but its perversion ; that which is born of love is the bliss of union, a sacred flame neither ignited nor fed by lust, for it is a condition of perfect equipoise. In the bliss of union all sense of duality is overcome : the two are one flesh because they are one spirit, and they are one spirit because the personal self, the nature of which is separative, is in abeyance : the least intrusion of the personal involves a return to the illusion of duality. The man and the woman, unified throughout their entire nature, dissolved in one another, the nemesis of unreality and unfulfilment at last absent, become as it were the bi-polar sexual organism of a greater being, and participators in a more abundant life.

In India this means of union with the universal spirit, this Yoga *à deux* in which each identifies the other with the opposite aspect of the self (*Âtman*), is called *Sahaja*. It has nothing to do with the cult of pleasure ; it more nearly resembles Tao, the path of non-pursuit : demanding nothing, denying nothing, desiring nothing, all is freely received and freely given in a reciprocity which is absolute and unconditioned. Such a perfect sex-relation is possible only to persons capable of cosmic or celestial love : possessiveness, pride, vanity, fear, shame, are all fatal to it, because these arise from the sense of I-ness. Celestial love is not self-love, but love of the Self through love of the beloved *as* that Self. It is an escape from the death-in-life of the personal self.

The ultimate effect of love of this order is to emancipate from the tyranny of sex through the development of bi-polarity in the individual:

> "Each shall be both, yet both be one."

The parties to such a relation instead of enslaving make one another free. The attraction which the sexes have for one another is rooted in this need—the need of each to develop its opposite within itself through feeding, so to speak, upon the opposite tincture in the other while at the same time feeding the other with its own specific tincture. For this is what occurs in the right relation between man and woman, the interchange being on all planes and in every part of their manifold natures. This is one of the things which every woman knows intuitively and every man must learn. As Katherine Mansfield says in a letter: "We are neither male nor female. We are a compound of both: I choose the male who will expand the male in me; he chooses me to expand the female in him." Through interdependence they win independence. This order of Yoga therefore has two phases: the giving of all to love and the leaving of all for love—for the enactment by each of the last act of the drama, which is between the self and the Self—the soul and God. And this last phase is a return to Raja Yoga, called "kingly" because it is the container of all other Yogas, which, transcended, one after another, leave only itself. This is because it is concerned solely with consciousness, the source and container of all faculties and all phenomena, the only enduring thing in a perpetually changing world.

IV

YOGA is of immemorial antiquity. There are many books about it, ancient and modern. The acknowledged masterpiece of this literature is The Yoga Sûtras of Patanjali. The date of its writing is unknown. The best occidental authorities place it at from eight hundred and fifty to three hundred years before Christ, though the Hindus themselves—who ought to know—ascribe it to a much earlier period. Even so, it is probable that Patanjali only reduced to written form teachings which had been transmitted orally for centuries.

The book is short ; its aphorisms are brief ; but it is packed with profound and subtle wisdom set forth in admirable order and detail. Its theme is the birth of the spiritual man from man physical—the theme of every sacred scripture. It is so great, so comprehensive and at the same time so condensed that one is tempted to say of it, as Omar declared of the Koran, " Burn the libraries for their value is in this book ! " But though clear it is also immensely deep, so that the books on Yoga have been for the most part commentaries on this one, for to ignore it is impossible.

Some claim that the best and quickest way to teach a person to swim is to plunge him suddenly into deep water. Following these tactics the author will now proceed to introduce Patanjali to the reader.

The Yoga Sûtras are divided into four sections or books. The first and second of these deal with the " right withdrawal " of the spiritual man from the veils and meshes of his psychic nature—the overcoming of mental habits and emotional moods. The third book is concerned with the " spiritual powers ", such powers being the natural mode of functioning of the spiritual man. Everyone possesses these powers to the extent that he is able to synchronize himself with the universal spirit: it is this tuning-in process which Patanjali essays to teach. The fourth book deals with the workings of that law the application of which to the individual brings the spiritual man to germination, growth, and flowering, from his material seed or sheath. First the object, then the means, then the method: the fourth book describes the method of release, hinted at in the final sûtra of the third book: "When the vesture and the spiritual man are alike pure, then perfect spiritual life is attained." The last part of this final book is in a way the mŏst important part of the entire treatise in that it reveals the true nature of the personality; were this placed at the beginning it could not be understood.

Keeping in mind this general outline, let us examine some of the sûtras in the order in which they occur, endeavouring to extract as much of their meaning as we can. A literal translation is impossible because it would be incomprehensible: a paraphrase embodying the approximate meaning is given instead. The author is indebted to Dr Jagadish Chandra Chatterji, the eminent Oriental scholar and author of *India's Outlook on Life*, for valuable help in the wording and interpretation of certain of the aphorisms.

(1) *Now then! Let us talk about Yoga,* Patanjali begins, the implication being that it is something which should be entered upon only after due preparation.

(2) *Yoga is the complete cessation of the activity of the versatile psychic nature.* Nothing is more revealing of the profound difference between Eastern and Western modes of thought with regard to these matters than this drastic attitude toward the "psychic nature" which here is assumed to embrace both the emotions and the purely rational mind. Soul-culture in the sense

of stimulating and making sensitive the emotions, and mind-culture in the sense of exercising the mere intelligence, are of slight efficacy in Yoga, according to Patanjali—at best they are but a means to an end, and should not be made an end in themselves.

(3) *When this happens the true seer in man manifests.* (4) *Heretofore it has been enmeshed in the activities of the psychic nature.* These activities, according to Patanjali, are five in number: *right knowledge, wrong knowledge, fancy, sleep, and memory.* He goes on to explain the nature of each, and how they should be dealt with.

(12) *The control of these activities comes through repeated effort of the will, and disinterestedness—the withdrawal of interest and its transfer to something higher.* He goes on to define disinterestedness:

(15) *Disinterestedness consists in the positive awareness of self-mastery on the part of one who has learned to overcome his thirst for sense-objects,*

6

whether actually perceived or only imagined. The achievement of this, according to the sixteenth sûtra, brings freedom from thirst for any mode of psychical activity through the establishment of the spiritual man. In the seventeenth sûtra Patanjali takes up the subject of meditation:

(17) *Meditation with seed goes through four phases: that which still retains an awareness of discursive concrete images; then abstract thinking, succeeded by the pure joy of comprehension of the universal ideation, and ending with the realization of individual being apart from and independent of such universal ideation.* Next he goes on to describe meditation without seed:

(18) *This form of meditation* (the seedless) *is that in which there is only the distillation of the essence of objectivity; that essence alone is there—produced by the repeated effort to experience complete cessation of all movement.*

Samâdhi, or super-consciousness, is of two kinds, a false and a true. In the nineteenth sûtra Patanjali says that the pseudo-*Samâdhi* state results from too much devotion to objectivity. He goes on to enumerate the qualifications necessary for the attainment of the true state of *Samâdhi*: (20) *The right form of Yoga is attained by means of confidence, courageous effort, self-awareness, self-concentration, and wisdom.*

In one of those sudden transitions which make the reading of the book a spiritual adventure, Patanjali turns from the consideration of union through knowledge and through will—Gnani and Raja Yoga—to union through love—Bhakti Yoga: (23) *There is another way of attaining the same end, nămely, by devotion to God.* And then he goes on to explain what he means by God: (24) *A God is that particular person who is untouched by any form of suffering, karma and its effects, and the subconscious clouding of the soul engendered thereby.* (25) *In Him the seed of omniscience present in everyone has reached its full fruition.*

In the thirtieth sûtra Patanjali enumerates the things which interfere with the development of spiritual consciousness: (30) *The barriers to interior illumination which drive the psychic nature this way and that are these: sickness, inertia, doubt, light-mindedness, laziness, intemperance, false notions, inability to reach a state of meditation or to hold it when reached.* No one should take up the practice of Yoga solely to cure sickness, but rather the other way round: he should gain health in order that he may so practise, as a runner tries to cure his lameness in order that he may enter a race. Certain bodily infirmities, however, like blindness and deafness, are not hindrances; by cutting off distractions they may even become a help. A bodily condition which holds the consciousness captive is the real handicap. The inability to reach a stage of meditation or to hold it when reached is due to mind-wandering. This is why the practice of concentration is so essential. The thirty-first sûtra continues in similar strain: (31) *Grieving, despondency, bodily restlessness, faulty breathing, also contribute to drive the psychic nature to and fro.* The thirty-second sûtra tells how to correct these psychic disorders: (32) *In order to avoid these things one should devote oneself to the realization of some single principle, for when it is fully realized all becomes clear.*

Suddenly, surprisingly, the note again changes in the following sûtra: (33) *Delight in the goodness of others, forgiveness of the sinful, lead to the quieting of the psychic nature.* Altruism is here prescribed as a principle of action leading toward liberation—the centring of sympathy and interest upon others. This is Karma Yoga; then follows Hatha Yoga: (34) *Or peace may be reached by the even sending forth and control of the life-breath.*

The next five sûtras indicate various methods of overcoming the wavering and perturbation of the psychic nature which make it unfit to transmit the inner light: (35) *Faithful, persistent application to any object, if completely attained, will bind the mind to steadiness.* (36) *As will also a joyful, radiant spirit.* (37) *Or the purging of self-indulgence from the psychic nature.* (38) *Or a pondering on the perceptions gained in dreams and dreamless sleep.* (39) *Or meditative brooding on what is dearest to the heart.*

The fortieth sûtra: (40) *Thus the whole universe is mastered,* brings this entire sequence to a close, the meaning of it being made clearer by the one which follows: (41) *When the perturbations of the psychic nature have all been stilled, there is a merging of perceiver and perceived.*

The first book dealt with the object of Yoga; the second book deals with its means: (1) *The practices which make for union are the discipline of the senses, the reading of the sacred books, and complete obedience to the Master.* The purpose of these practices we are told is *to bring soul-vision and to lessen suffering.*

The hindrances or distractions are five in number: *ignorance, self-assertion, desire, aversion, and attachment.* Of these ignorance is the chief, and the source of all the others. In this Patanjali is at one with Buddha, who said: "All sin is ignorance." In the fifth sûtra ignorance is thus defined: (5) *Ignorance is taking the non-eternal, impure, evil, and non-*Âtma, *to be eternal, pure, good, and* Âtma.*

Next we are told how to deal with these distractions. (10) *These distractions when they*

* M. N. Dvivedi, in his commentary on this sûtra, has this to say: "The shortest explanation of ignorance is taking a thing for what it is not. It should, however, be remarked that it does not imply mere privation of knowledge as the word *Avidyâ* may suggest. It is a positive mental state which induces the result of taking a thing for what it is not. It is neither one of the instruments of knowledge (*Pramâna*) nor an absence of them, but a something apart from them all. When there is no *Avidyâ,* the instruments of knowledge, the thing to be cognized, and all similar distractions, are reduced to naught, and one sole unity, all knowledge and bliss, is the result. Hence it is easy to see that ignorance is neither one of the instruments of knowledge nor apart from them, but it is in fact that thing by which the original unit appears threefold, as cognizer, the cognized, and the instrument of cognition."

have become subtle are to be removed by a counter-current. That is, ignorance is to be overcome by insight; self-assertion by self-abnegation, desire and aversion by indifference to what is pleasant or unpleasant, and attachment by non-attachment. (11) *Their active turnings are to be counteracted by meditation.* This is the key to the entire regenerative process, for meditation is purification.

Next follows an analysis of the cause of sorrow, which is rooted nowhere save in the psychic self: (15) *To the enlightened all personal life is misery because of its anxiety, its restlessness, and because all its activities war on one another*. There is no cure for this misery save in the transformation of the psychic nature, achieved through a steadfast utilization of the "means of Yoga."

In the twenty-ninth sûtra, which rightly understood is an entire scripture of itself, we are told what these means are: (29) *The eight means of Yoga are: sympathy and compassion towards all, observance, posture, control of the life-currents, withdrawal, attention, contemplation, absorption.*

It will be noted that these divide themselves naturally into two groups, the first five being concerned with the world without—one's relation toward others and the development of the physical man—and the last three with the world within—spiritual development. Patanjali then proceeds to tell all that is implicit in each of these "means."

The first one (*Yama,* untranslatable into English) involves the abstention from (30) *killing, falsehood, theft, fornication, and greediness*; terms which should be interpreted to include meanings far deeper than their dictionary meanings, however. What is meant by killing is enmity of any kind toward anyone: one should not only not tell lies, but should honour every truth by use. Theft is not only illegal appropriation, but the desire for any kind of illicit gain; incontinence includes the kind referred to by Christ—*whosoever looketh on a woman to lust after her.* Greediness is every kind of grasping and embraces not only coveting, but keeping anything beyond the necessities of life.

These are called vows or commandments. They are absolute, and universally obligatory at all places and in all times. The *observances,* which are given next, are relative only, being subject to modification in conformity to differences of custom and variations of character and temperament: (32) *The observances* consist of *contentment, austerity, self-study, and submission to God.* The necessity for this relativity is apparent, for what is austerity to one person or in one state of society is self-indulgence in another; some are incapable of self observation while others are too self-analytical; different gods are worshipped in different times and in different countries. Therefore all that is required is conformity to the observances within the limits of the practicable and possible.

The first two means of Yoga are disciplinary and initiatory; they give the moral strength and resilience necessary for the practice of the next three, which are physiological.

Of the third means of Yoga, which is "posture", Patanjali has this to say: (46) *Right posture should be firm and without strain.* In this and the following sûtra there is manifestly a twofold meaning; though the instruction has reference to physical posture—the insistence upon the importance of which is a constant characteristic of all Yoga teaching—the word should be construed to mean not only a position of body easy and erect, but an analogous attitude of mind which shall give strength to resist "the shocks of infatuation and sorrow."

The next aphorism, (47) *By relaxed effort and complete mastery of the endless,* should be read as part of the preceding. The two constitute the only Hatha Yoga instruction in the entire book, but it is enough. " Meditation on the endless " may mean the fixing of the mind upon the Eternal, but it refers also to the *Kundalini,* or coiled-up serpent fire, the arousing of which within the body prematurely is attended with so much danger that it is only spoken of in this ambiguous way. Patanjali says here, in effect, what has been said elsewhere at greater length in this volume, that with right posture, right meditation, and " relaxed effort " the endless coil of the *Kundalini* will bestir itself at the right time and in the right way so that it shall emancipate and not devastate—for there is a saying, " It gives liberation to Yogîs, and bondage to thieves."

Prânâyâma, the right control of the life-currents, is dealt with in the forty-ninth sûtra and the one following: (50) *The life-current is either outward, or inward, or balanced; it is regulated according to place, time, number; it is prolonged and subtle.* This sûtra is intentionally obscure, for *Prânâyâma* is something which cannot be taught in text books, and its practice is fraught with danger. The little which has been said about it elsewhere, however, will provide the needed clue: In-breathing should be slow and deep ("prolonged and subtle"), retention should be sufficiently protracted to thoroughly aerate the blood-stream; expulsion should be gradual, one nostril being used for inhalation and the other for exhalation ("place"), a period being established for each ("time"), the said period being regulated by counting ("number").

The final sûtras of the second book are concerned with the disengaging of the powers of the spiritual man from "entanglement with outer things": (55) *Then follows perfect mastery over the senses*. The earliest known use of the word Yoga, which occurs in the *Upanishads* has exactly this meaning—the " harnessing " of the senses.

The third book is the Book of Spiritual Powers. These are powers inherent in the spiritual man ; and as the perturbations of the psychic nature are successively stilled they come more and more into activity. In the same way that the personal man is an *inversion* of the spiritual man, so are the faculties and powers of the former inverted spiritual powers —self-seeking is an inversion of *Self*-seeking. The major portion of the third book is devoted to an enumeration and description of those spiritual powers which are as it were the by-product of " perfectly concentrated meditation." Their résumé will not be attempted here for the reason that the acquiring of these powers should be no concern of the novice ;

spiritual rebirth should be his controlling motive.

To the true Yogî these powers are not valued for their own sake but only as milestones marking his progress. Patanjali himself declares, (37) *These powers are obstacles to the highest spiritual vision.* They should never be regarded as an end in themselves.

The same thing is true of the beauty of the bodily vesture of the spiritual man, which is described thus: (46) *Shapeliness, beauty, strength, the temper of the diamond: these are the endowments of that body.* To undertake the practice of Yoga for the purpose of acquiring power or becoming beautiful is to put one's head in the lion's mouth: the *motive* behind an act or a course of action determines the issue with an absoluteness impossible of comprehension by minds unaccustomed to perceive as the cause of all-differentiations differences *in consciousness.*

The sûtras of the fourth book are particularly brief and cryptic. They deal with what might be called the *technique* of release—the transfer of powers from one plane to another, from one vehicle to another; for man is like an electric transformer which changes the character of a current, steps it up or steps it down.

(2) *The transformation of one form into another is possible only by a resolution into a primary state and a re-constitution into the form desired.* (4) *Vestures of consciousness are produced by identifying oneself with them in thought.* By these means the same consciousness may manifest in diverse forms, and (5) *In the different fields of manifestation the consciousness, though one, is the effective cause of many states of consciousness.*

Like electrical energy, which may manifest as power, light, heat, or what not, consciousness, however many and diverse its manifestations, is unalterably *one*: the will, mind, and emotions, man physical, astral, mental, are but different aspects of one consciousness.

(6) *Among states of consciousness that which is born of contemplation is free from the seed of future sorrow*. It is the desire-nature which engenders karma and brings about repeated rebirths. *Samâdhi*, the state of consciousness born of contemplation, is desireless, therefore "free from the seed of future sorrow."

(7) *The works of Yogîs are neither white nor black—make neither for bright pleasure or dark pain. The works of others make for pleasure or pain, or a mingling of both*. This also is on account of the desirelessness of the Yogî: he can remain aloof even from his own actions —be both actor and disinterested spectator and critic. As said before, only the action prompted by desire brings fruit of pleasure or pain.

(11) *Since the dynamic mind-images are held together by impulses of desire, by the wish for*

personal reward, by the substratum of mental habit, by the support of things desired; therefore, when these things cease, the self-reproduction of dynamic mind-images also ceases. Because man is a projection or " ray " of the Self, he partakes of Its essential nature, and therefore possesses the power of self-determination—free will. In the exercise of this he falls a victim to his own self-created mind-images, as one may become frightened at his own shadow, or deceived by his own image in a glass. This brings about a self-torment which leads ultimately to the discovery that the source of his sorrow is in himself—" the wish for personal reward, the substratum of mental habit, the support of outer things desired." Exercising anew his divine prerogative of self-determination he *changes* his consciousness in the sense *of restoring* it, whereupon the reproduction of dynamic mind-images and their attendant torment comes to an end.

(18) *The movements of the psychic nature are at all times subject to observation, since the Spiritual Man who is lord of them remains unchanging.* The fact that one is able to observe his own emotional perturbations and mental processes shows that he is himself that witness and watcher which is the spiritual man.

(22) *When the psychic nature takes the form of spiritual intelligence by reflecting it, then the Self becomes conscious of its own spiritual intelligence.* This is one of the most profound and illuminating of all the sûtras in that it gives a glimpse of the process whereby consciousness becomes self-conscious, which is by *reflection,* just as a woman learns of her beauty in a looking-glass. The psychic nature is the *mirror* of consciousness: cleansed, it reflects—"takes the form of"—spiritual intelligence. Thus the Self becomes conscious of Itself.

(23) *The psychic nature, taking the colour of the Seer, and things seen, leads to the perception*

of all objects. When calmed and clarified by contemplation the psychic nature, like clear, still water, reflects true images, just as when that nature is disturbed and muddied by desire, everything is confused and distorted.

(24) *The psychic nature, which has been printed with mind-images of innumerable material things, exists now for the Spiritual Man, building for him.* The psychic nature, "sown in corruption, reaped in incorruption", once the tyrant, now the slave, like Shahrazade now brings delight and profit to her sultan, the Spiritual Man.

From the twenty-sixth sûtra onward Patanjali essays to explain the nature of final emancipation: With knowledge comes the cessation of the desire to know; the Yogî attains to the supreme state of non-attachment in which all transformations come to an end, having fulfilled their purpose, and he enters into the bliss of pure being: (34) *Pure spiritual life is, therefore, the inverse resolution of the potencies of nature, which have emptied themselves of their value for Spiritual Man : or it is Awareness established in its own state.* All life is spiritual life : in its centrifugal, or *evolutionary* aspect there is the manifestation of that which is inherent ; in its centripetal, or *involutionary* aspect, there occurs " the inverse resolution of the potencies of nature, which have emptied themselves of their value for Spiritual Man." Consciousness, become self-conscious through the contemplation of its self-created images, returns to its pristine state or condition. It is upon this note that the book ends.